THE INVISIBLE ARM OF PEACE

THE INVISIBLE ARM OF PEACE

Poems by
Khairi Hamdan

Translated by Katerina Stoykova

Accents Publishing • Lexington, Kentucky • 2022

Copyright © 2022 by Khairi Hamdan
All rights reserved

Printed in the United States of America

Accents Publishing
Editor / Translator: Katerina Stoykova
Cover Image: Photo by Javardh on Upsplash

Library of Congress Control Number: 2022938140
ISBN: 978-1-936628-93-3
First Edition

Accents Publishing is an independent press for brilliant voices. For a catalog of current and upcoming titles, please visit us on the Web at

www.accents-publishing.com

CONTENTS

Introduction / vii

Sudden sunset, as if a blade ... / 1
Shrapnel of Memory / 2
To Live / 3
Return to yourself slowly ... / 4
Deception / 5
When I shattered the mirror ... / 6
In the fruit basket remain three lemons ... / 7
My Neighbor / 8
He Embraces You Even Without Arms / 9
Between the fingers ... / 10
A step toward the sky; ... / 11
Nothing is as usual ... / 12
A Promise / 13
Don't Bow Your Head / 14
Green as Never Before / 15
I Speak of You and Me / 16
During the stretches of time ... / 17
Suffering Suits the Human Race / 18
I shared with a stray wave ... / 19
It's beneficial to hold ... / 20
The Wisdom of the Iceberg / 21
Survival Training / 22
Damned to Oblivion / 24
Silence is the invisible arm of peace ... / 25
I can pass through a needle's eye ... / 26
Optimism / 27
Portrait of Sin / 28
You know I've erected a sandcastle ... / 29
I don't want the wind ... / 30
Where I come from ... / 31
I gave my daughters ... / 32
Hasn't Arrived / 33
Forecast / 34
It is a punishment to be heard and understood ... / 35

There Are No Random Chrysalises / 36
Date at Border Patrol / 37
Laconic and categorical like a steam hammer ... / 38
Anxiety / 39
Anxiety / 40
South of Everything / 41
Camps Sprouting in the Sky / 42
Go To Sleep! / 43
Awakening / 44
The cloud rests upon my shoulder ... / 45
Violating the Rule Book / 46
But This Is Out of Context / 47
The Bedouin stood at the fair's exit ... / 48
Dead Zone / 49
According to the Poet / 50
What outlasted the flood? ... / 51
Do Gods tire? Asked the ant ... / 52
Prayer / 53
Sin and Forgiveness / 54
Dervish / 55
On the seventh day ... / 56
Times of Passion / 57
I, the Bedouin / 58
Dream / 59
Lick your wound with the blade of the night ... / 60
Another Last Supper / 61
As the drops of water ... / 62
A Proper Poem for a Wakeful Death / 63
Answer Yes or No / 64
Compass / 65
On the scales—mind and heart ... / 66
Unwittingly, for the duration of our lives ... / 67

About the Author / 69

About the Translator / 69

INTRODUCTION

I met Khairi Hamdan at a literary event in Bulgaria, where he is a well-known poet, writer and translator. He has had an unusual life. Khairi was born in the city of Dier Sharaf on the West Bank of the Jordan River, but he grew up in Jordan after his family emigrated there in 1967. In 1982, he moved to Sofia to attend university and to study engineering, and in Bulgaria he found another country to call his own. He married a Bulgarian woman, became a father of three daughters, and mastered Bulgarian, one of the languages in which he now writes poetry and prose.

I have read a number of Khairi's poetry books in Bulgarian, and I have selected a few of my favorite poems to present to the English-speaking reader. In these poems you will find the sand of the Sahara Desert, the Bedouin, the Dervish, and unmediated conversations with God. You will encounter destroyed temples, refugee camps, border patrol, children with nontraditional names. You will also find lyrical poetry of intimate tenderness and the unrelenting drive to be a better human being.

I hope you enjoy seeing the world through Khairi Hamdan's eyes, for it is rich and compassionate, and our world is a better place for having Khairi Hamdan's poetry in it.

Katerina Stoykova

★

Sudden sunset, as if a blade
callously slices the day,
stirs ancient sadness, blended with prophet blood.

And the sand rises—golden pearls in the calendar,
organizes the constellation into chaotic matrix.
Only the beasts meekly fall asleep.

Sudden sunset subdues the senses of its will,
injures and rejoices the footprints of eternity.
Time alone remains awake.

SHRAPNEL OF MEMORY

I try to gather
residual fragments of exile.

I draw a runaway but don't fly out.

I draw a train
with fixed wheels.

I draw a fake cloud—
floats in the sky but
carries no rain.

I draw blind eyes,
lips—parched,
palms—trembling.

I draw poetry and song.
I invent a singer,
pianist, violinist and a …
mountain climber—
together to harvest a dream.

TO LIVE

When early in the morning you open your eyes,
before peeking out the window,
before coffee,
before the first cigarette—
reach toward your chest.
Don't fear the consequences.
Press your palm. Without fear of consequences.
Check if your heart
is still beating.
If you're still alive.
Perhaps you're a corpse,
perfectly proficient
at the art of living.

★

Return to yourself slowly,
softly knock on the front gate.
Don't rush into the living room or the bedroom.
Check your pulse; you might be missing,
and instead of you, a gang
of random drifters may have settled in.
Don't rush to return to your tent.
Allow your previous selves to enter first.

DECEPTION

The night's too tight for all of us.
The first to depart were the oldest ones.
Those who remained at twenty forever,
rushed to make love again.
Then the wisest left.
Those who remained at thirty forever,
relentlessly sought new ways of salvation.
And the most beautiful ones, at forty,
departed at once,
with an immense desire to count the stars.
Just you and I stayed, deceived by the night,
which entirely belonged to us,
just like the pier, the city, the skyline, the semaphore,
the last wrinkles of the sofa, and
the residual stanzas of lore.

★

When I shattered the mirror,
I saw many faces.
Why didn't the moon
reflect an image of you
despite my appeals?
After surviving another morning,
I harkened back to the hum of the universe.
I didn't rush to open my eyes
before learning the name of the ant
passing by my front door.
She greeted me and smiled
before continuing on her way.
One day she might accept
my invitation for a cup of coffee.

★

In the fruit basket remain three lemons
and a package of dates.
I also have enough poems, stories and parables.
I have much sin—
as much as the human condition could encompass.

From the available ingredients,
please try preparing
a pastry for two.

MY NEIGHBOR

I know my neighbor,
modest and quiet,
a hunter and a pirate.
At times unwise—volatile,
but it's enough for a cloud to pass by,
for him to smile,
to wet his hair,
to sense the rhythm of the day,
to take a pill just in case,
for God,
for forgetting,
for entertainment.
I know my neighbor—
modestly and silently he lays in my chest,
surrounded by worries, ribs and veins.

HE EMBRACES YOU EVEN WITHOUT ARMS

The man who lost his arms in a desperate battle
waves to you again and hugs you even without them.
Nobody notices, however,
that the span seems narrower by a meter and a half.
The man did jump with a parachute
but forgot to open it.
So he plummeted into the abyss with such abandon
that the birds envied him.
At last he had discovered how to fall
into the sky, counterclockwise,
counter to the hand of the clock
which long ago stopped reporting
the rare moments of revelation and passion.

★

Between the fingers
of an inanimate cliff
grows a sand rose,
grow gypsum and barite.
On the grape harvester's shoulder—
a jar of aged wine.
The baker's forehead is
engraved with morning,
his shirt and tank top
smell of loaves.
On the way to your bed—
thorns, a lonesome moon,
a rudderless bike,
scattered pages
from a dictionary.

★

A step toward the sky;
a cloud, passing on the other side, applauds innocent intentions.
The sun douses in a tub and abdicates,
neither rises, nor discovers its horizon.

Another step toward you,
time hobbles, the seconds outrun the hours.
Eternity is but a nap, and the temple lacks candles.
Homeless sleep inside the library; there is a revolt before the parliament.

The dream dons daytime garments,
lights up a cigarette, another,
drinks an extra cup of coffee, and then consciousness falls dormant.
The game continues in front of the ancient theater,
and the sergeant boldly proclaims: Check and Mate!

★

Nothing is as usual.
The sky is different,
the winter—a disguised summer.

Nothing is as before,
time is a broken shoulder.
Home relocates between your braids.

Nothing is translucent,
the wall embraces your warped shadow,
the wet sun suddenly drowns.

A PROMISE

Toss the carnation
into the sea.
There is no vase,
nor direction. Also,
the thorns are tamed.
Another wave,
frothy water
a delinquent
pledge.

DON'T BOW YOUR HEAD

You can force the sun
to crawl in your shadow,
the moon—to carry your bags
as you travel.

Contrary to all the laws of physics,
I ignite every time when
with my waters I water your gardens,
put out fires, you.

GREEN AS NEVER BEFORE

Suddenly I'm overcome with desire to soar,
to thumb through others' notebooks,
to sense the cool dawn, the bitter wine.
And as I was freely and timidly plummeting,
I tore an autumn leaf off a proud fig.

Unceasing desire to embrace your shadow
that just passed through,
covered with a light shirt and a shawl,
and on your face—traces of grass.

A tired yellow walnut tree flew by.
I picked a flying fig leaf
during a time of rest and absence,
yet my heart—green, green as never before.

I SPEAK OF YOU AND ME

She placed a hand on his shoulder
before hot tears sprang out of his eyes.
I speak of the shoulder.

He lowered his head, pondering-
the darkened morning, the barefoot bread.
She embraced him and caressed his forehead.
I speak of the warm palm.

He couldn't contain the flow—
the ghost house flooded.
Submerged also were the shop,
the municipality and the church.
I speak of the missing link
between sky and earth,
I speak of God.

We met on a suffering boat
with no rudder nor mast, no direction nor compass.
We were rescued by a poem, a sudden scream,
A rainbow, ascended in the sky.
I speak of you and me.

★

During the stretches of time
the senses stay alert
and the clock ticks off presence,
I open the window
of my personal desert,
where I rarely allow human beings.
I discard the heart, the kidney, the quill,
traces of incinerated memories,
your lipstick, the echo of your steps—
approaching then quickly receding.
I discard the ink and the dictionary.
I lose consciousness and fall asleep.

SUFFERING SUITS THE HUMAN RACE

Bitter sugar, unconsumed, lacking passion,
begets a sweet memory of a former storm
at the bottom of a coffee cup.
Handwritten on a colorful booklet
are two travelers' names:
she—local, he—a foreigner who arrived
some time ago on a wandering boat
and stayed until the next promise.
The foam eats up the ink, the first letters survive,
a brief poem and a place to reunite.
Next year—same time, same pier.

Salt asserts its nature
in the wound, merciful and raw.
The flesh belongs to another.
That summer God descended,
caressed us with the comb of death,
sedated his faithful prophets.

Suffering suits people.

★

I shared with a stray wave
a few innermost truths
about the seduction of the sea's bottom.
We spoke about you, as well.
How during another hot summer
our hearts remained chunks of ice.

★

It's beneficial to hold
a chunk of ice between your palms,
to squeeze this petrified tenderness.
Inside you, the Iceberg melts, embarrassed.

THE WISDOM OF THE ICEBERG

While melting,
the iceberg realizes
that the night consumes its darkness,
the day—its light,
without mercy the rivers gulp
the waters of a wandering iceberg;
the fig tree
does not reach for its fruit.
If ungathered by human hands,
this fruit decays in the lap of its mother.
All the while
the glacier wisely continues
to wither.

SURVIVAL TRAINING

I.

I train my heart to withstand thirst,
to beat in times of tranquility,
when blood skips the veins
and heads for the heavenly pillar.

II.

We seal the transition
to the dead seasons of love and hate,
rush into reality.

III.

Love is a lesson for those advanced
in the philosophy of survival.
Love teaches how to accept winter—
the tired face of summer.

IV.

The sun beams beyond the clouds,
and the grains of snow are simply feathers
of a freshly bathed angel.

V.

Your flesh, your essence is a celebration,
unexpected wedding in my soul.
Do you sense the vibrations of our crossing
into a wet space,
into a cloudy misunderstanding?

VI.

Render your rainbow with a flute
and leap into the dark.
Countless fireflies rush around you.
Darkness changes garments in your honor
and immediately bounces from you.

VII.

I smell of coffee, not of rakia,
and I'm as awake as a decomposed corpse.
Wine is my bridge between being and nihilism,
said Khayyam before embracing the sky.

DAMNED TO OBLIVION

As if you haven't kissed lips at sunrise,
haven't strolled until dawn's early hours
holding the hand of Venus,
just popped out of the sea.

You're damned to oblivion
as if you haven't protested, haven't revolted
against the fierce winds,
against the human gene for power
and the oppressive presence of autumn.

You're damned to oblivion
as if you haven't chased trains, flights,
haven't cried after a faint silhouette,
as if you haven't read the Iliad, a few holy books
or you haven't felt
a thousand and one aches, yours or not.

You're damned to oblivion
as if you weren't a letter
in the book of creation.

★

Silence is the invisible arm of peace.
Stillness is the unending roar
of death.
Silence is the essence of desert,
stillness—its tough punishment.
Everyone has the freedom to choose
between roar and peace.

★

I can pass through a needle's eye,
beyond a lonely cloud—
a guard inside the sky's ulcer.

I can pass through your slumber,
to touch your day, your dream.

But I could hardly touch
the roof of the pain you sow
everywhere around me.

The world needs no more
bandages for boxing, for horses,
for new sexual positions,
for Olympic games.

No need for undue efforts
for excessive passions.

OPTIMISM

Don't apologize. Stockpile sins.
Convenient clouds don't rain to order
and southern winds sometimes blow from the North.
The sea, even knee-deep, portends death.

PORTRAIT OF SIN

Do you know the boy
who sought salvation for his soul
at various points around the world
dressed in a thin smile,
barefoot to the last cell of his internal blaze?
Do you know him?
The same one who fell into an ocean of passion
and the sharks refused to devour him
even though he downed half of the water
of the Mediterranean sea
and is still thirsty—
thirsty like a widow
for supple lips,
for generous bestowing of femininity,
for greater faith in dawn.
Somewhere high above the dreams,
close to the nanosphere,
the boy still walks barefoot,
dressed in nothing but a lifeless smile.
He begs the blue whale
to swallow him for a moment.
To fall asleep for an eternity
in the name of forgetting,
so that he may exist in a future time—
like a newborn prophet
in the kingdom of sin.

★

You know I've erected a sandcastle.
In it I keep a few secrets and childhood memories.
I invited the sea for a visit, to drink a glass of seawater
or wine and to spend a few nights with me.
That's how I flooded the castle, that's how I ended up homeless.
So what? I'd invite the sea again, even the ocean,
despite that I can't swim.

★

I don't want the wind
to lift me up,
I simply crave wings.

I don't want honey in my cup,
I simply desire the bees not to lose direction
but to return to their hives.

I don't want fireplace and hearth.
I covet abundance of sun
to brighten the heart,
the pigeons before the church,
the vagabond by the frozen fountain
and my mother's grave.

★

Where I come from,
the moon sobs and bathes in sand.
Where I come from,
the souls of the dead join the waves
and in God's name emigrate
in the direction of the gale.

Where I come from
rest the bones of two people
who once fell in love
so I could exist.
In my dreams I return to that place,
collect shrapnel from my battles,
raise a white flag,
and fall asleep.

★

I gave my daughters
the vintage comb
with its Mediterranean breath.
With it I used to attempt to tame
my curls, wild
as if they'd grown in a minefield.

HASN'T ARRIVED

The train hasn't arrived.
It derailed in an unidentified direction
and resumed its travel towards the blueness.
Farmers, artists, lawyers and doctors ride,
run away from their daily lives, protest lies,
rivalry, fame and unrequited love.

The train will not arrive, the station manager announces,
don't wait for puffing wagons, noisy greetings, vanity!
The reasons for the engineer's revolt are countless—
loneliness, low pay, frayed nerves,
lack of spare parts, search for alternative space,
banquet in first class, wedding in second,
birthdays of two travelers without seats,
improvised court, unpostponable case, urgent surgery.

Dear citizens, don't wait for the slow train,
originally expected a bit after midnight!
The runaway train seeks an alternate destination,
seeks a desolate station where painful confessions
and premature forgiveness are sanctioned.

FORECAST

Rainy.
The forecast is probably kidding—
it feels clear, quiet and sunny.
So what!
Lonely clouds stroll about,
perhaps searching for their wet tails.

Windy.
The forecast is deceiving us—
it feels foggy, and the wavy sea
relentlessly transmits encoded messages.
Perhaps it seeks its other half on land.

Recent.
Though it feels distant, unreachable and gloomy …
So what?
Perhaps having depleted their polite words,
the stars in the sky are committing suicide.

Bullets louder than applause.

★

It is a punishment to be heard and understood,
yet to have the world turn its back on you.
Nobody needs naked truths.
At the flea market
the semi-truth trade is flourishing.

THERE ARE NO RANDOM CHRYSALISES

We've met repeatedly, randomly
by a railroad,
at a cross examination
in a Latin-American
or Middle eastern prison cell.
We recognize each other.
You always appear elegant,
no makeup,
fleeting and majestic.
You measure precisely
only the weak tones of the heart.
You lead me to the well
harboring poets.
There they bathe
under the same denominator.
Again and again you state
that poets always perish
during spring,
turn into chrysalises,
and later take flight
as free butterflies.

DATE AT BORDER PATROL

We'll get together soon—I said—
in a moment, a second, a year, a century,
after one more migration
of stupefied birds, ready
to pay again the due
in front of the grey door
of the border patrol.
The parched lips of the day,
the sleep, dissipated between fleeting nightmares,
the directions, aching for road signs
quicken the encounter of the species.
A bored wanderer, a dispirited artist
who drew God on the back
of an empty box of cigarettes.

A thin blade separates
north from south.

Painful embraces,
damp kisses,
crumpled sheets,
bitter coffee,
we sink into the bastion
of the grim daily routine.
We'll get together—I said—
at the edge of the cliff,
next to the slippery step
at the entrance to the cave.

★

Laconic and categorical like a steam hammer,
the homeless wounded wolf rests in others' dreams,
services his needs with another's hands.

The homeless wolves recline on the heavenly dome,
stare at the lock to the afterlife.
They don't allow nicknames, care for their own skin.
Gray, vicious and free, they howl against the watchful city.
The feral silent beasts peer into the dark.

They don't fall asleep, they don't fall asleep!

ANXIETY

What would we do
if suddenly
our beloved enemies
vanished from our lives
and before the gates
of our dreams
our hateful friends
comfortably settled,
masked,
with pale smiles?

ANXIETY

You forgot your memory
locked in a drawer.
Who needs an ID?
The policeman smirks twice.
An arrest follows.

SOUTH OF EVERYTHING

It's South everywhere—
boredom, delights,
desperate prostitutes,
bitten lips, tattooed mornings,
lack of dreams, only rancid fish.

South of the world banks,
of the border police,
of the punctured paper boats
and rusty trains—
a crowd of kids
without traditional names,
or addresses.
They kick the skull of faith.

South of everything—
another cemetery
sprouting in the place of
a just-demolished temple.

CAMPS SPROUTING IN THE SKY

I'm not skilled at planting seeds
over the parched earth
that God deserted
before completing His work.
The harvest begins,
the branches hang heavy
with the fruit of fear.
Since God willingly left Palestine,
tent camps sprout
even in heaven.

GO TO SLEEP!

Go to sleep!
The city nods off,
suffocates inside its own slumber,
wakes in wee hours
before sunrise,
as the moon smokes its last cigarette.
The city nods off,
as I lower the blinds
before the late news
announcing the demise
of another dream
supported by the government coffer,
guzzled at the crossroads
between east and west
on the shore of a forsaken ocean.
Sleep, my city!
A journey awaits you,
a serenade awaits you,
a relentless roar.

AWAKENING

I woke up early this century.
I continue sleeping.

As usual I downed my coffee
with medication and poetry.
I continue sleeping.

As usual I went to work:
Hello, dear angry colleagues!
The metaphor is missing—
I continue sleeping.

Someone lit the wick of a new year,
of a new war.
I continue sleeping.

The White House erased
my homeland from the world map.
I continue sleeping.

I feel no pain, nor commiserate
with the migrating birds—innocent citizens
with no permanent address.
I continue sleeping.

I look around.
Everyone treats the new century
in their own way
and in their own way
everyone continues sleeping.

★

The cloud rests upon my shoulder;
the rain has been postponed
until the second awakening.
The bells toll at five steps till eight.
To the east there is no more west,
to the south—abundance of sun and sand,
enough to warm up the northern nights.

VIOLATING THE RULE BOOK

Inadvertently I broke the rules.
So many cracks in the constitution!
I violate the first article of the treaty of silence.
I'll reveal the truth of the original fruit
and the snake will be fully exonerated.
There will be a lack of guilty parties
until the second coming.

According to fortunetellers and crooks,
I'm a few inches shy of reaching you, as much as a desert,
but in a vacuum the choice is tricky,
slippery,
ruthless.
I choose not to choose
and to remain semi-free.

My anarchic heart senses another tornado.
I can neither reach the stem of my primordial desires,
nor safely return to myself.

BUT THIS IS OUT OF CONTEXT

After eternal absence, the ship arrives.
The masts—broken, the lifeboats—lacking,
but that's out of context for this story.

The ship is packed with illegally captured whales.
They share their amazement, their sudden amnesia
using an incomprehensible earthly language,
but that's out of the context of the enigma.

After another leap in time, I discover
that I ride the blade of oblivion's wave,
but that's outside the context of this poem.

The train, by some miracle, still rides on the rails.
Panting engine, exiled passengers, shattered windows.
The machinist abandoned his holy post ages ago,
but that's outside the context of the revelation.

★

The Bedouin stood at the fair's exit,
offering handfuls of sand
that he'd patiently collected
from a nameless desert
while living in a tent
with anxious ancient souls,
with ghosts and tacit cliffs.

The day was passing in wait.
One child gathered the courage
to buy a handful of sand
instead of a greasy pastry,
and during the entire night,
ceaselessly talked with the sky.

DEAD ZONE

God's place of death—
a dead zone.
The necropolis is split in two.
On one side
tower tiles, engraved
with suras from the Quran.
On the other side—quotes
from the Bible, and a cross.
On the right—a minaret.
On the left—a bell.

And the corpses decompose
equally fast.

ACCORDING TO THE POET

Here is the truth according to the poet:
he released a drop of honey into the dam
and for a week already the water tastes sweet.

Has anyone considered
what might happen
if the artist, in God's image,
tossed a pebble into the sea?

★

What outlasted the flood?
The sand dunes emigrated,
lost their genetic compass.
The desert became the new Amazon.
Flocks of birds sail under the soil of the earth.
Faceless shadows rise inside us,
the ones who survived another ordeal.

★

Do Gods tire? Asked the ant
and went on shouldering its load.

A few tons of wheat and corn remain.
Meanwhile, humanity continues
to squash ants and to mate.

PRAYER

God,
You, who ride the blue tent
and rotate the seasons,
you, who thrash around
the obedient clouds,
the rebellious sands,
the unending gales,
share with me your innermost teachings
before death manages to strike me.

He looked at me and said:
Son, first you must learn to lose,
to suffer.
Find salvation
on a crestfallen ship.
Plunge naked into my waters.
Rise above your pain.
Down a glass of water with a handful of salt.
Swallow the seeds
of resurrection.

SIN AND FORGIVENESS

As I was saying goodbye, mother, I picked a fig
from your ageless garden.
The olive tree with its deep roots
turned and wept without a sound.
Only one butterfly heard its sobs …
and I left, swam in unfathomable waters, mother.

I forgave my past,
I forgave the sprouting wheat,
the kite, abandoned in my childhood room.
I gave forgiveness for the broken windows of memory,
for the incident to be born
during plague.

And before the eternal sunset appears,
I'll face him, the almighty creator.
I'll timidly whisper in his ear:
Forgive. For God's sake, forgive.

Ahead lies an imminent encounter with the green universe,
with my desert, which awaits, biting lips.
Ahead lies an imminent meeting with you, honorable father,
and with you, beloved mother.

DERVISH

Forgive me, Mullah!
Forgive me for turning to you
with such delay.
You haven't seized for a second
whirling in the right direction,
reeling the universe toward yourself.
You ceaselessly believe,
rediscover salvation
in the doom and contagion.
Forgive us, Mullah,
that unlike you, we lost
patience and balance,
that we circle solely
around an insignificant,
lone moment.

★

On the seventh day
immediately following creation,
while Your Lordship decided to take a breather,
man stirred,
shook the throne,
then again approached you for forgiveness,
waiting for the eighth day.

TIMES OF PASSION

I master hands, dream of carpets,
paint wind, feign joy,
raise a slogan, take down two.
So much poetry and not a single poem.
So much water with no sea
and an array of embraces with no love.
I build a bridge, destroy a lonely city,
until the next suburb,
until the next merciless famine.

The street has turned into a home,
the electric post—into a night light,
the car horns—into alarm at dawn.

Today was sunny with spring weather.
Today was yesterday, rainy and cold.
The city is place, the city is time.
Tomorrow will be today
without a doubt, without a watch.
Time dictates its own rhythm.
We're all seconds in the diaries of God.

I, THE BEDOUIN

The desert is unfathomable—
sometimes sweet,
more often—hostile.
The camel is watered,
well-fed, its hump
swells with dignity.
She carries me and the dog,
the dog is feeding fleas.

Before the next haze
I glimpse the mirage
of a yellow traffic light
at the backdrop of a sea of fine sand.
We descend world upon world,
riding the hump
of the universe.

The camel gives me, the Bedouin,
a co-conspiratorial glance.

DREAM

I dreamed I played the saxophone
in a packed auditorium lit by chandeliers,
after which I woke up
and departed for the desert.

The rain has many names,
the sky—just one: Blue.
Take off your soul,
leave it on the hanger.

★

Lick your wound with the blade of the night.
Don't try to apologize to anyone.
Rise above the roof of the world.
Circle the nanosphere and higher.
Let God realize that you exist.
The glass wall of the universe
stands fragile and transparent.
Climb it, find your corner
and leap again into the abyss,
where your shadow awaits—
everlasting dry mist.

ANOTHER LAST SUPPER

What's God seeking at my place?
I don't hide prophets in my tent.
Christ's cross remained in Rome with Pilate.
Mohamed's mantle stayed in Istanbul.
Solomon's cane has been corroded to its core.
But despite all earthly passion and suffering,
in my humble hut I also entertain revered guests.
History repeats its moves,
issues invitations to another last supper.
And I'll find somebody whose lips to kiss.

★

As the drops of water
quietly trickle into the creek,
so imperceptibly our days flow out.
Is there time for a brief respite,
a hug, a flirt?
Life imperceptibly depletes
its potential.
And what to do now
that we've reached
another crossroad?
There is time for a sip of air—
the butterfly would say,
just before blazing in the light.

A PROPER POEM FOR A WAKEFUL DEATH

Beyond the shadow of the limitations
of the available languages, doubts and faith,
I sought a possible exit beyond,
beyond the silence of the birds
and the roar of yellow Sahara sand
rolling through my veins.

Peer into the third eye of the day.
Can you glimpse even for an instant
the dried-up tear inside a wet iris?

Still, try waking in your dream
while you're light years away from the wakeful death.
Don't inquire into the technology of the quickening rhythm
even if you suffer from hypertension.
Eternal life has been conserved
in the extinguished myth of the lighthouses.

The dead are the last to insist on a burial,
the duty-free zones for crossing beyond have been quarantined.
God opens so many heavenly gates.
Awake consciousness is needed for profound enlightenment.

ANSWER YES OR NO

Answer yes or no
when death abruptly swoops in and asks:
Are you willing to pause your earthly journey for a brief eternity?
It is a privilege to be alone with death,
the benefit of having such a choice
happens only once.
For as long as you are able,
answer every letter arriving over the local airways
before you become a bit of the universal dust and peace.

Answer the call of the flute—
the lost impulse of the absent poets,
the incomplete painting, the unrained cloud,
the prophecy of an upcoming confession—
answer the call, the flute brings relief.

The streets exhale their emptiness,
recover their former dreams,
light up unfinished cigarettes,
invite drifters, mentally ill, outsiders and gentlemen
to jump in puddles.

And before midnight I will walk on the trembling road of the flute
and hummingbirds will bless my next flight.

COMPASS

At times the baggage arrives
before the traveler,
the captain loses
another compass.

At times he goes mad,
embraces a white shark,
sobs on the pectoral fins
of a dolphin.

The body is a vulnerable suitcase of skin,
the train is an insidious snake,
the ship is a soulless goddess.

A storm and a hurricane arise.
Somewhere rage Monsoon and Mistral,
and the directions often lose
their purpose.

★

On the scales—mind and heart.
Unequal race with the light,
seeking someone's beginning and never an ending,

On the scales—heart and mind.
Unequal race with love,
seeking many beginnings, sometimes even an ending.

★

Unwittingly, for the duration of our lives
we seek safe corners
to store our final wishes—
words, prayers and loves.
Unconsciously, we choose our endeavors.
The epilogue chooses us.

ABOUT THE AUTHOR

Poet, writer and translator Khairi Hamdan was born in 1962 in the city of Dier Sharaf, on the West Bank of the Jordan River. In 1967, his family emigrated to Jordan, where he lived until 1982. Since then, Khairi Hamdan has lived and worked in Bulgaria. He is the author of a number of books published in Bulgarian and Arabic, most recently the novel *Chestnut Gardens* and the poetry collection *The Water Lilies of Memory*. Hamdan translates poetry and prose between Arabic and Bulgarian and has been awarded several international honors for his translations, as well as for his original work.

ABOUT THE TRANSLATOR

Katerina Stoykova is the author of several award-winning poetry books and the Senior Editor of Accents Publishing, where she has selected, edited, and published close to 80 poetry collections. Katerina acted in the lead roles in the independent feature films *Proud Citizen* and *Fort Maria*, both directed by Thom Southerland. She splits her time between the coast of the Black Sea and the rolling hills of Kentucky. Katerina writes, lives and thinks in two languages.

www.ingramcontent.com/pod-product-compliance
Lightning Source LLC
Chambersburg PA
CBHW030200100526
44592CB00009B/367